WoofiLeaks

ISBN 978-0-9970009-0-0
First edition

Printed in the United States of America.

Cover and layout design by William van Roden
Chapter washes by Gillian MacLeod Haspray

WoofiLeaks™ is a trademark of
Emmerling Communications LLC.

Special discounts available on quantity purchases.
For details, contact publisher@WaterBowlPublishing.com

Water Bowl Publishing
215 East 68th St., Suite 5E
New York, NY 10065

WoofiLeaks
Your Dog's Secrets Revealed

Written and illustrated by
John Emmerling

WATER BOWL PUBLISHING

DEDICATED TO MAX, THE WISE—
AND FUNNY—DOG WHO ALLOWED
ME TO SHARE MY BED WITH HIM

CONTENTS

INTRODUCTION

Max walked up and wagged his tail for attention.

"I plan to write a book," he said.

"Great," I said. "A novel?"

"Nothing so frivolous," he scoffed. "As a service to mankind, I'll be leaking some secrets."

"What kind of secrets?" I asked.

"Dog secrets," he said. "Like why dogs sniff hydrants, why puppies pull on the leash, what makes dogs so funny."

"Don't dogs have a code of silence?" I asked.

"Actually, yes," admitted Max. "But our silly taboo has lasted centuries—time to lift the kimono."

"Sounds good," I said. "Wish I could help."

"Well," said Max, "you do type faster."

 —John Emmerling

CHAPTER 1
Quirky Secrets

Why do dogs sniff hydrants?

My friends pee at the plug

It's our neighborhood spot

When I log into a hydrant

One sniff tells a lot

Like what mood Duke is in

When did Beau have a look?

Fireplugs are no mystery

They're the canine Facebook

Why do dogs love the beach?

Here's a metaphysical answer
That all dogs understand
The beach is a launchpad
Felt when paws hit warm sand

On the beach we will rocket
Like the birds, we will fly!
On the beach, your house rules
They will never apply 🐾

Why do dogs chase balls?

Mother Nature doesn't make

An exact—and perfect—sphere

You might ask about the orange

But that fruit has faults severe

Throw an orange, it rolls flat

Hugs the grass, sticks like glue

But your rubber ball goes fast

And it bounces high—*Wa-hooo!*

Why do dogs scream for ice cream?

I admit this one's odd

Ice cream's cold and it's slick

You'd think for dog palates

Frozen treats wouldn't click

Ice cream's secret is *sweetness*

When dogs lick it—can't stop!

I've been thinking 'bout openin'

The first McDog ice-cream shop 🐾

Why do dogs growl?

All dogs are born friendly
And stay sweet while a pup
So when you hear that first growl
You might wonder what's up

Dogs growl as a WARNING
They can sound like a hornet
If their growl turns to *growwwllll!!*
Best advice—do not scorn it 🐾

Do dogs have favorite TV shows?

Of course we have favorites
Shows with dogs are must-see
Downton Abbey's yellow Lab
Was a beauty, dogs agree

But we hated that *Mad Men* jerk—
Tossed his Irish setter out
Hey! If *Scooby Doo* is casting
Maybe you know a talent scout?

Which car do dogs prefer— sedan or convertible?

Dogs are experts on cars

Cuz all cars speak to us

They're a zillion times better

Than a trip on a bus

A long drive makes our day

In a hardtop—noses out!

But a ragtop adds sunshine

So that's our vote—with a shout!

CHAPTER 2

Puppy Secrets

How does a puppy choose you?

Here is how all puppies think
When choosing a home for life:
They want a place that's happy
They don't want noise and strife

If a pup comes up to you
Speak softly—nuzzle and touch
Put a twinkle in your eyes
And *Bingo!* Doesn't take much 🐾

How should you paper-train a puppy?

Puppies piddle without stop

Making puddles 'round the house

If you lay a paper down

They'll avoid it, will not douse

Here's a secret you should try:

Dip paper in the piddle

Put it down for pup to sniff

Next piddle goes in middle!

Why does your puppy pull on the leash?

Every puppy when it's born
Is told by Puppy Mother:
"You must guard your master well
Tough job you will discover

"People walk without a care
Talking, texting on their phones
So PULL HARD—watch out for threats
Zooming skateboards can break bones!" 🐾

Why do little kids love puppies?

Kids and puppies start out small
Then they grow up together
At first the pups learn faster
But kids catch up, get clever

Pups and kids agree on stuff
Chase balls and play with toys
Puppies make the PERFECT pals
Sharing love, and licks, and joys

Should your dog welcome a new puppy?

Your dog is devoted

You get a hundred percent

Yet a new pup's such fun

Any dog would consent

But puppies need training

So your dog's job will expand

You'll get MUCH LESS attention

(Sure hope you understand)

CHAPTER 3

Secrets of the Dog-Human Relationship

Are dogs really happy when you come home?

When dogs hear your key click

We leap up to our feet

Dash fast to the door

Get there first for a greet

And does this make dogs happy?

I'm delighted to say

Every dog answers: YES

Cuz you're home—time to play!

Do dogs think they look like their owners?

Human legs are too long
And you only have two
Your nose is scrunched up
And your skin's the wrong hue

Your ears look like seashells
Your mouth seems so shrunk
(If I did look like you
I'd go off—be a monk)

Why do dogs want to sleep in your bed?

It's too bad that you spent
Twenty bucks at Wal-Mart
For that bed with big bones
And a red woofing heart

But a dog's job is to guard
To keep masters in sight
So we snooze up against you
One eye open all night 🐾

Why do dogs beg at the table?

When people dine on roast beef

Juicy steak or lamb chop

Dogs suffer *plate envy*

Then start begging nonstop

A dog's bowl can be boring

Sometimes filled with stale grits

While the meals you consume

Could be served at the Ritz!

Why do dogs look sad when you go out?

At the door, dog tails droop

Tiny dog tears are shed

We invented "The Sad Look"

To play games with your head

If I want a new dog toy

Your RESISTANCE must wilt

The Sad Look opens wallets

Cuz you leave oozing guilt 🐾

CHAPTER 4

Possibly Disgusting Secrets

Why do dogs sniff other dogs' butts?

It's just sociable, that's all
Like when humans shake hands
Except when palms grip so tight
Your germs discover new lands

The dog "hello" is pristine
We sniff butts—never touch
No germs jump between us
But your handshake? Too much! 🐾

Why do dogs hump legs?

We learn watching masters

In your beds around two

We see you hump-bumping

While you bill and you coo

But my humping is playful

Not sexy, not slick

I mean no harm to your guests

It's a greeting—and it's quick! 🐾

Why do dogs roll in stinky stuff?

When dogs flop on a dead thing
We want its smell laid on thick
Cuz rolling in stinky stuff
Is an ancient wolf trick

If my wolf-self goes hunting
Say I'm stalking a moose
He'll be fooled, just smell tuna
But I'm a sport—let 'im loose

Why do dogs rub butts on expensive rugs?

This happens to dogs
Just a few times a year
When an itch starts to itch
Our southern hemisphere

If the itch drives us crazy
We drag butts 'cross the floor
Could use an old bathmat
But our butts like silk more 🐾

Why do dogs fart silently?

When humans pass gas

The noise can be loud

With a BAM! or a POW!

Your farts startle a crowd

We dogs prefer whispers

A silent *pfffft* spreads perfume

Noses wrinkle, fingers point

Dogs smile—leave the room

CHAPTER 5

Uncharted Territory Secrets

How many barks do dogs have?

Eskimos have fifty words
To describe the types of snow
Dogs have something like that:
Twenty barks for mistletoe

A low bark means "Watch out!"
A high-pitched bark: "Let's run!"
Can't bark all TEN THOUSAND barks
'Fraid that'd break my tongue

How big is the dog vocabulary?

Start listing the words
Your dog knows while a pup
You'll get more than one hundred
When done counting them up

Adult dogs are loquacious
Most could earn a degree
(I've been thinking 'bout Harvard
For my "P" "h" and "D")

Can dogs smell a billion smells?

Human noses are feeble

Have so few "smelling cells"

Our noses—forty times more!

(Why we're cursed by drug cartels)

Put a dog's nose to the test

He'll detect a MILLION whiffs

But dogs cannot smell a *billion*

Did a cat tell you that myth?

Can dogs hear a pin drop two blocks away?

Although dog ears are keen

Let's not be absurd

When that distant pin drops

Its "ping" could sound blurred

But our ears are amazing

Hear a thousand tones you can't

Want to listen to some?

You'll need an ear transplant 🐾

CHAPTER 6

Healthy Living Secrets

Can dogs sniff out disease?

All things have a smell
And all smells are unique
If each *disease* has a whiff
A dog's nose it can seek

We have sniffed tiny cancers
Dogs can tell if you're ill
Our hunches can alert you
(And there's never a bill) 🐾

Will having a dog make you live longer?

This is certified truth
Not a tale told by Grimm
Daily walks with your dog
Are like trips to the gym

This routine is terrific
For heart, liver, and spleen
Of course you'll live longer!
I'm your exercise machine 🐾

How many baths do dogs need— really?

Dogs will jump in a lake

Run through rain for a soak

Mother Nature's our bathtub

But your tub? It's a joke!

The thing's ugly and bulbous

And you use it too much

So how 'bout ONE BATH a year . . .

Or two baths, in a clutch?

Why do dogs sleep so much?

Out of twenty-four hours
A dog's sleep demands plenty
Counting afternoon snoozes
Prob'ly comes out to twenty

Our sleep is important
You should know this up front
We grab winks when we can
Must stay sharp for the hunt 🐾

CHAPTER 7

Gotta-Go Secrets

How should your dog tell you it's poop time?

There is no standard poop sign

So watch what you feed

If you give greasy scraps

Nature's call comes with speed

But when raised on good food

Dogs invent a "Right Now!" hint

It's unique, so learn it well

Avoid the frantic poop sprint 🐾

Why do boy dogs lift a leg to pee?

We stroll up to the pole

Raise our legs to the sky

Let fly with a stream

And we're hopin' for high

Macho pride is behind this

Cuz when "yellows" get matched

If my mark tops 'em all

A block legend is hatched 🐾

Why do girl dogs squat demurely to pee?

Female dogs I have known
Are fastidious and neat
When it's time to relieve
Girls are very discreet

They hunker close to ground
And this really does matter
Cuz while boys spray the landscape
Girls want minimum splatter 🐾

Why do dogs circle before they poop?

Do you need to know this?

It should be private—our poo

Would you stare while I dump

If I were a gnu?

Okay, here's why dogs circle:

We must find a clear spot

Need to stake our own claim

And only then will we squat

CHAPTER 8

Official Secrets— Canine High Command

What is the official dog position on neutering?

Now really!—How'd you feel

No ifs, ands, or buts

If I came with some scissors

And snipped off your nuts?

And I grieve for all bitches

(In that word's canine use)

When vets un-plumb their plumbing

And make cold their caboose

What is the official dog position on being man's best friend?

Poets use it in poems
Authors write it in journals
"Man's best friend is a dog"
Even posted by colonels

Dogs cherish this friendship
You're my bestie forever
And don't worry 'bout setbacks
Dogs stick with you—whatever

What is the official dog position on giving a paw?

It's the first trick we do

As a puppy in your house

And since it still thrills you

We give a paw, never grouse

But the paw trick's mundane

Puppy entry-level stuff

Why not ask for some Shakespeare?

Or a math quiz—make it tough! 🐾

What is the official dog position on wearing costumes?

Please listen up, people:

All pets hate this stuff

From dogs, cats—parrots, too

Comes this stinging rebuff

We ABHOR silly costumes!

So want clown, shark or bunny?

Then get out your checkbook

It'll cost you big money 🐾

What is the official dog position on barking at mailmen?

Sure, mail carriers work hard
Slog through snow, sleet, and rain
Some even bring dog treats
But that's a P.R. campaign

We're barking at JUNK MAIL!
Cuz people buy such dumb gear
Like that horrid pink leash
(My pals still laugh and sneer)

What is the official dog position on being a pack leader?

We invented "Alpha Dog"
A phrase we use for boss
Humans plagiarized our term
A theft that makes us cross!

Alpha Dogs are born to lead
We firmly take control
Alpha Men? They're wannabes
Fit for second-fiddle role 🐾

What is the official dog position on keeping animals in ZOOS?

What gives humans the right

To put animals in jail?

Are you so high and mighty

You'd lock up a blue whale?

Seems to us you're misguided

Filling zoos with God's creatures

Just leave 'em be in the wild

And set up some bleachers 🐾

CHAPTER 9

Profoundly Secret Secrets

Do dogs fall in love with other dogs?

When love happens, you'll see it

Dog hearts flip in a beat

Could be dachshund or mutt

We just met on the street

We cherish our dog friends

But here is the thing

Sometimes this love fades

Might just be a fling

What makes dogs so funny?

We start out as puppies
Practice yucks we can lob
And when people adopt us
Jokes are part of the job

Dogs are born to be funny
(Seen my stand-up routine?)
If you tested my DNA
You'd find a comedy gene

Are dogs smarter than cats?

Now this question is touchy
(I have a friend who's a cat)
So let's google "Who's smarter?"
Which head gets the pat?

You'll find dogs ranking high
Up with chimp and with whale
But the cat is—sorry, pal—
Farther down on the scale 🐾

Can old dogs learn new tricks?

You can bribe any young dog

Cuz a pup is a rookie

They'll do a new trick

For a crumb of stale cookie

But old dogs have wised up

Our new tricks are for sale

(I'll entertain for prime rib

But make it rare, served with ale) 🐾

Will your dog always love you?

This question is puzzling

Cuz folks really should know

A dog's love never stops

It's a constant warm flow

Dogs love you through thick

Dogs love you through thin

Our love is ETERNAL

(And that's truth—without spin) 🐾

NOTE: IF YOU HAVE
ANY DOUBTS ABOUT
THE ACCURACY OF THIS
BOOK, MAX WOULD
LIKE TO REMIND YOU OF
HIS LIFELONG MANTRA:
"IF A DOG SAYS IT,
YOU CAN BELIEVE IT."

ACKNOWLEDGMENTS

Max is over the moon with thanks and gratitude for these helpful humans.

DRU-ANN CHUCKRAN Editorial wizard—a dog-loving creative collaborator who was with us from the book's beginning.

WILLIAM VAN RODEN Brilliant book designer—constantly surprised us with cool graphics and breathtaking page designs.

GILLIAN MACLEOD Marvelous illustrator and talented designer—painted those big color-splashy chapter pages.

MICHAEL DEWEESE Digital illustration whiz—taught a pen & ink guy the joys of cartooning with Photoshop CC.

JONATHAN EMMERLING John's creative director son—proposed secrets, added gags, directed Max's YouTube video.

MIKE PETERS Creator of doggish comic strip *Mother Goose & Grimm*—his tips gave "Cartoon Max" attitude.

FRAYA KATZ Max's NH breeder—an ever-flowing fountain of dog info & insights.

DR. DAVID EDELSTEIN Fact checker—and inspired *New Bark Magazine,* pg. 77.

PETER FRUMKIN Digital craftsman and production guru who tackled Max's debut book—made the pages shine.

PENNY SANSEVIERI Indie publishing sage took young pup of a book, nudged it into a scary world.

NORTON GARFINKLE, WARREN ADLER, KENNETH ROMAN, MIKE SLOSBERG, JIMMY BORYNACK, BILL GRIFFITH, AND ALAN SILBERSTEIN *The Lobster Lunch Bunch*—our monthly "innovation" lunch, all members cheered Max from the get-go.

Max also licks the faces of these friends, supporters, and trusted advisors: Patrick Armitage, Chuck Divak, David Elliott, Samantha Emmerling, Sam Garvey, Mariana Hoppin, Rich Kelley, Barbara King, Bridget Marmion, Louise Peabody, Betty Sargent, Jeniffer Thompson, Reed Thompson, Solange Thompson, Michael Van Patten, Kyle T. Webster (and his magical digital brushes), Alan Zwiebel—and Max's beloved great-grandniece, Molly.

In conclusion, Max sends a universal WOOF OUT to people everywhere who *believe* dogs were put on earth to calm and bring sanity to the worst aspects of humanity. So far, this canine project is a work in progress.

CPSIA information can be obtained at www.ICGtesting.com
Printed in the USA
BVIW12n0235151016
465103BV00002B/5